Water

Words by David Bennett
Pictures by Rosalinda Kightley

A BANTAM LITTLE ROOSTER BOOK

TORONTO · NEW YORK · LONDON · SYDNEY · AUCKLAND

More than half the world is covered by water.
Most of the water is in our oceans and
is very salty.

You can play in the oceans, but you cannot drink the water.

The water you use every day is not salty. It is fresh water, and you could not live without it.

You use lots of water every day . . .

. . . when you drink,

... when you wash,

...and when you brush your teeth.

Where does all the water you use
come from?
Rain from the sky fills up lakes and
rivers and also collects under the groun◄

Water is pumped from the rivers
to a huge man-made lake called a reservoir.
The water is kept there until it is needed.

The water is cleaned to make it safe
for you to use. Then it is pumped along
big underground pipes to your home.

Water helps us do many things . . .

. . . wash clothes and dishes, cook our food,

. . . clean the car, and water the lawn.

Wild animals help themselves to fresh water wherever they can. Fish cannot live out of water at all.

Plants also need water to live and grow.

Sometimes rainfall is not enough.
Then plants must be given extra water.
The vegetables you eat need
lots of water.

You can't hold water between your fingers.
But when water gets very cold, you can.
It becomes frozen and is called ice.

Even rivers and lakes freeze.
When raindrops get very cold,
they turn into snow or hail.

As the weather gets warmer, the ice and snow melt and change back into water.

Sometimes this happens too quickly.
Too much water can cause a flood.

Water also changes when it gets very hot. Boiling water turns into steam. You can see steam coming out of a pot on a hot stove. You must never go near boiling water.

In summer, heat from the sun can dry up
rivers and reservoirs, and there is less rainfall.

Some parts of the world don't get enough water because it almost never rains. But where most of us live, the rivers and reservoirs fill up again by spring.

If you are careful in and around the water, the games you play will always be a lot of fun.

You can paddle and swim . . .

. . . sail boats,

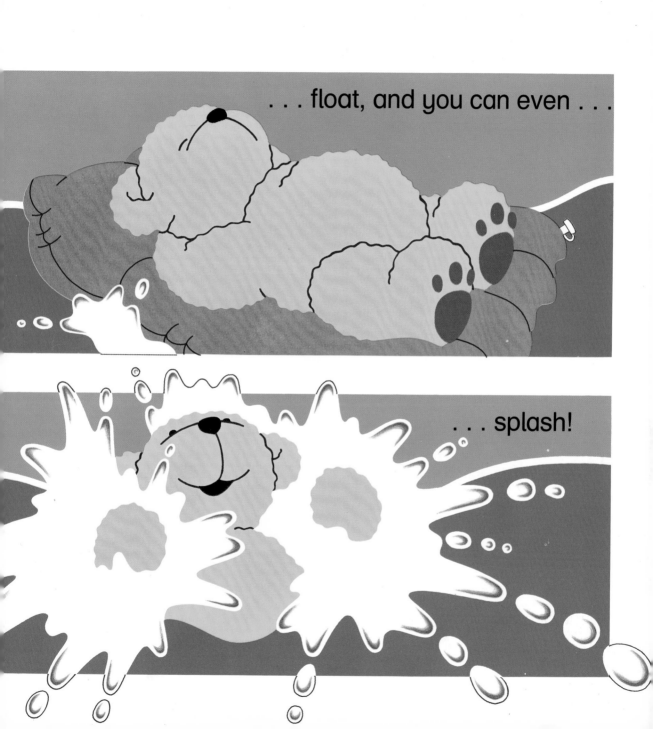

BEAR REVIEW

1. More than half the world is covered by water.

2. The water in our oceans is salty. The water you use every day is fresh.

3. You could not live without water. All animals and plants need water, too.

4. Water can change the way it looks. Very cold water freezes into ice. Very hot water turns to steam.